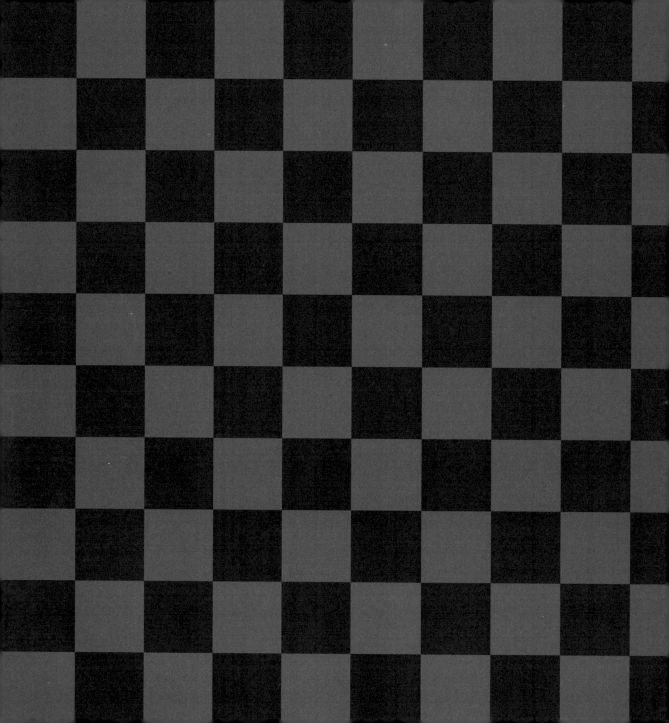

BLACK & WHITE

DOGS

EDITED BY J.C. SUARÈS

CollinsPublishersSanFrancisco

A Division of HarperCollins*Publishers*

First published 1992 by Collins Publishers San Francisco

Copyright © 1992 J.C. Suarès

Captions copyright © 1992 Jane R. Martin

Additional copyright information page 80

All rights reserved, including the right of reproduction in whole or in part in any form.

Designed by Jennifer Barry

Picture Editor Peter C. Jones

Library of Congress Cataloging-in-Publication Data

Suarès, Jean-Claude.

Black & white dogs /edited by J.C. Suarès.

p. cm.

ISBN 0-00-255081-4

1. Photography of dogs. I. Title. II. Title: Black and white dogs.

TR729.D6S83 1992

779'.32—dc20   91-45974

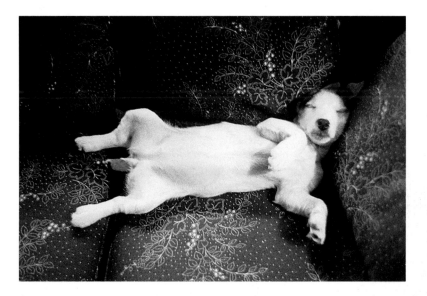

ROBIN SCHWARTZ
Susi, Jack Russell Terrier Pup, 1984

*A*rt and photography tell us something about the evolution of our relationship with dogs over the past 200 years: once mere employees in the hunting and herding trades, today they are family, intimate of hearth and home. Before the age of the great eighteenth-century portrait painters, dogs appeared mostly in court and hunting scenes. Velázquez and Titian included dogs in their paintings, but only as decorations, not as members of the royal families they painted. It was not until 1775, in a turning point, that Joshua Reynolds first showed a child in an embrace with her dog. "Miss Jane Bowles, aged 3" was not a member of the aristocracy, but rather the daughter of a well-to-do family of merchants. Other artists of the era expressed their love of dogs as well. William Hogarth included Trump, his pug, in his self-portrait. Thomas Gainsborough, who never missed a chance to include dogs in his paintings of the English upper class, was especially fond of Pomeranians and is said to have painted "Bitch and Puppy," featuring two fluffy white animals belonging to the musician C.F. Abel, in exchange for viola lessons.

The earliest examples of photography pick up where the painters left off. Dogs are being hugged by children in the first daguerreotypes, shot in photo studios along lower Broadway in pre-Civil War Manhattan. When the camera could travel, dogs and children were at play, or asleep together on straw mattresses. When the camera became available to anyone and wallet-size snapshots could be printed, dogs took their place in the family of man forever.

Photography, most of it black-and-white, is key to understanding our love affair with dogs throughout the latter part of the nineteenth century and most of the twentieth. We've seen dogs at play, but also at the jobs they perform: firehouse dog, sled dog, army dog, watch dog, circus dog, Hollywood and lifeguard. We've seen them go to war, rescue people from avalanches, cross the Antarctic, and clown around in commercials. We've seen them in the company of ordinary people, as well as in motorcades side-by-side with the most powerful leaders of the century: think of F.D.R. and Falla, Nixon and Checkers, Bush and Millie. Such memorable black-and-white images remain embedded in our collective psyche.

The only thing that has changed in the past hundred years is the cost of dog friendship. Your dog's ancestors got table scraps and an occasional bone. The 1860s marked the advent of manufactured dog food, with the introduction in England of the dog biscuit. Today, a pup's life entails an average expenditure of $4,400 for a daily feast of meat by-products, poultry by-products, seafood by-products, feed grains, and soybean meal marketed under a host of brand names your dog will never know.

Where once upon a time the family dog was occasionally washed with laundry soap in a tin tub (and not before he got very ripe), today you can pop in for a shampoo and blow-dry at emporia like Château du Chien in New York ($30) or Judy's in Los Angeles ($40). TIME magazine warns that a recent five-day hospitalization for a golden retriever in Washington, D.C. set the owner back $1,036.40, including $140 for a liver scan. If you live in Chicago and worry about your dog running around loose in the back yard, Business Week reports that for $12 per day you can drop it off at A Dog's Life, a new dog day-care center.

Inquire of most dog owners, though, and they'll hardly flinch at the costs of dog care. Dogs are entitled to the best because they are members of the family. No wonder a recent study shows that 5 percent of the 16 billion pictures we take each year are of animals. That's a lot of wallet-size photos.

J.C. Suarès

A N D R É K E R T È S Z
The Concierge's Dog, Paris, 1926

Like the super in a New York
apartment building, a Parisian concierge plays multiple roles:
fixer, protector,enforcer, and snoop.
The dog suggested those traits to Atget, though it's unlikely the real
concierge lived above the ground floor.

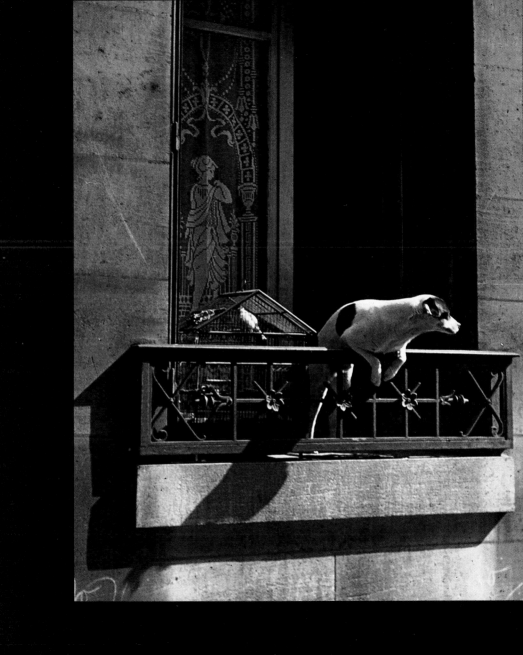

PHOTOGRAPHER UNKNOWN
Violin Child, c. 1930

*"I found this in my grandmother's photograph
album. It may have been taken in Milton, Massachusetts,
but no one knows for sure."*

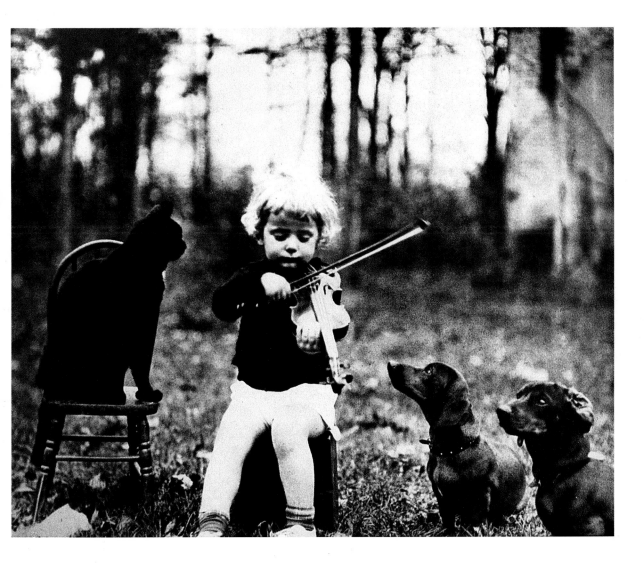

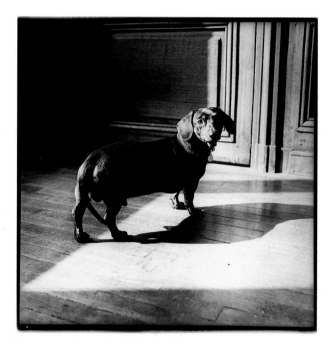

PETER HUJAR
Above: *Archie Warhol*, 1976

Andy Warhol's beloved miniature dachshund holds court in the oak-paneled dining room at the artist's Union Square studio.

■

EDWARD STEICHEN
Right: *Dorothy Parker*, May 1932

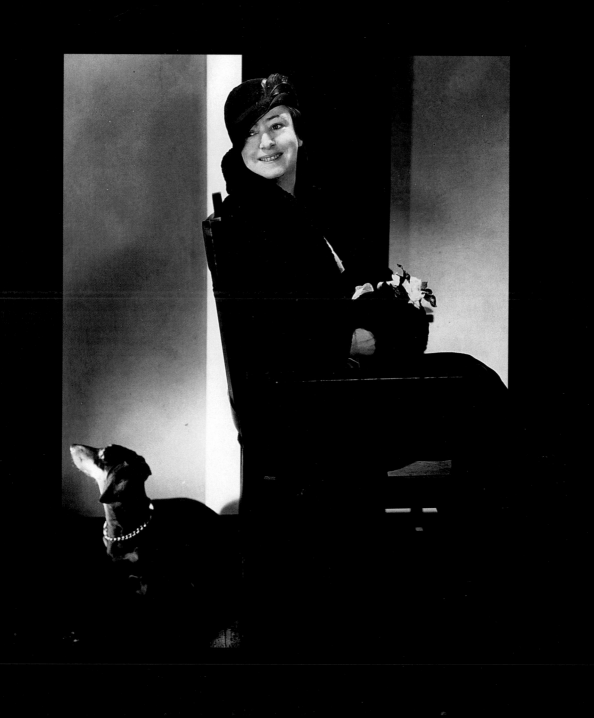

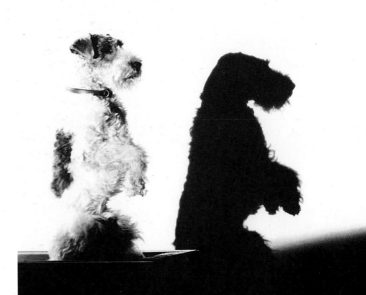

PHOTOGRAPHER
UNKNOWN
Scene from Song of the Thin Man
c. 1947

"Teamed again," offers the caption
to this staged publicity still,
"William Powell and Myrna Loy
are reunited in their favorite screen roles
as Nick and Nora Charles in
MGM's Song of the Thin Man,
the latest of the wisecracking
detective adventures ... with Asta, the
Thin Man's pooch, also lending
a helping paw." Actually this dog is a
successor to the wire-haired fox
terrier, Skippy, who originated the role.
Skippy also starred in "The Awful
Truth" and "Bringing up Baby."

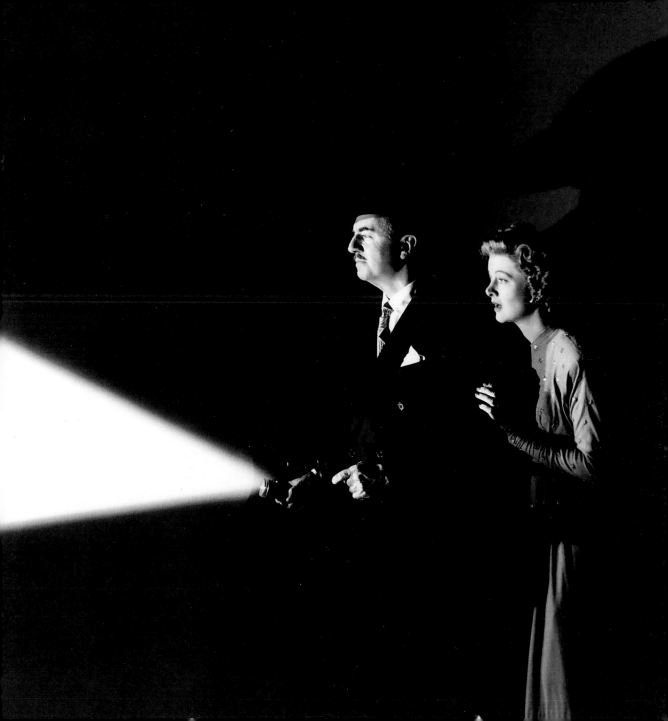

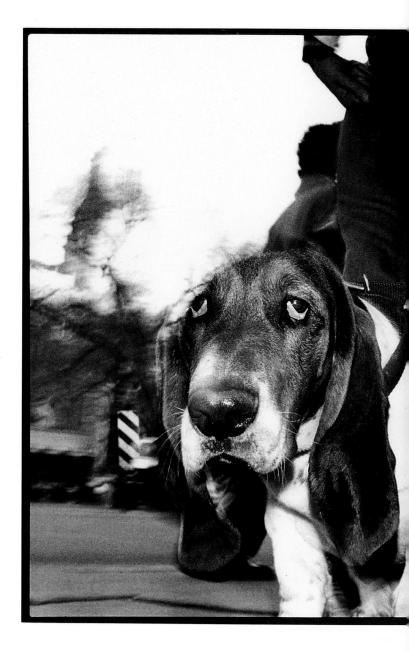

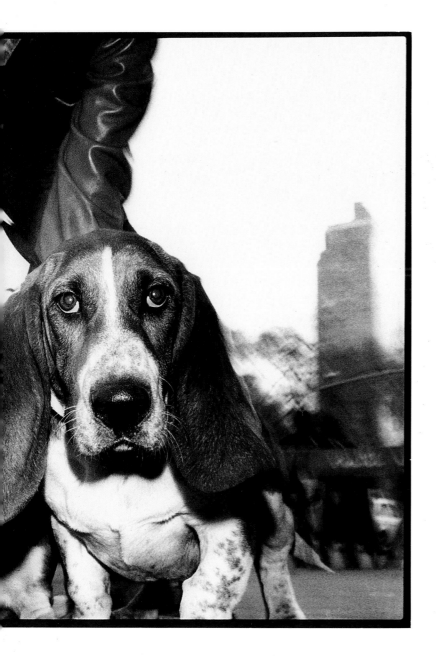

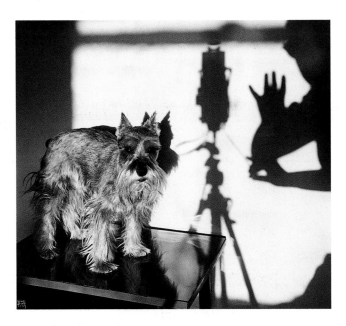

ILSE BING
Above: *Shadow of Me and My Camera*
While Studying Staccato, c. 1948

During a session in Bing's
New York studio, her schnauzer strikes a stoic pose.

■

ANDRÉ KERTÈSZ
Right: *Study of People and Shadows*, 1928

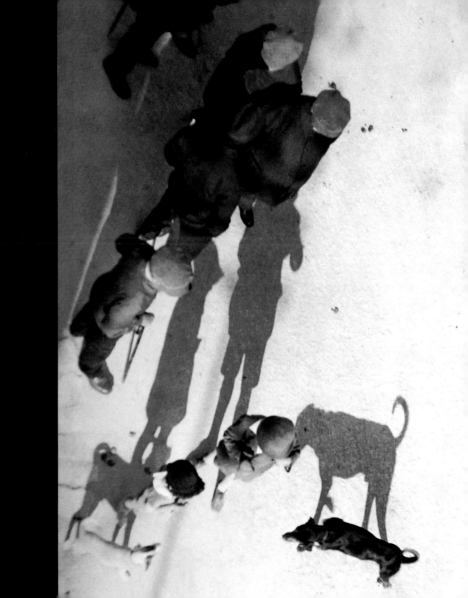

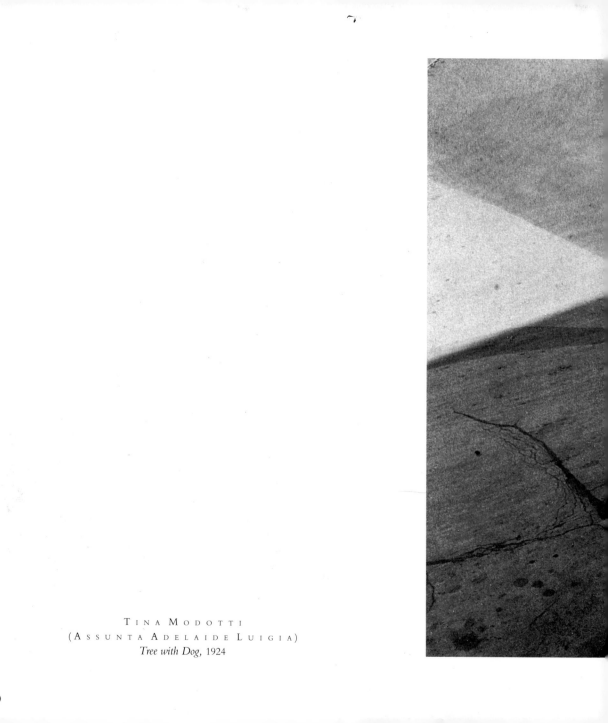

TINA MODOTTI
(ASSUNTA ADELAIDE LUIGIA)
Tree with Dog, 1924

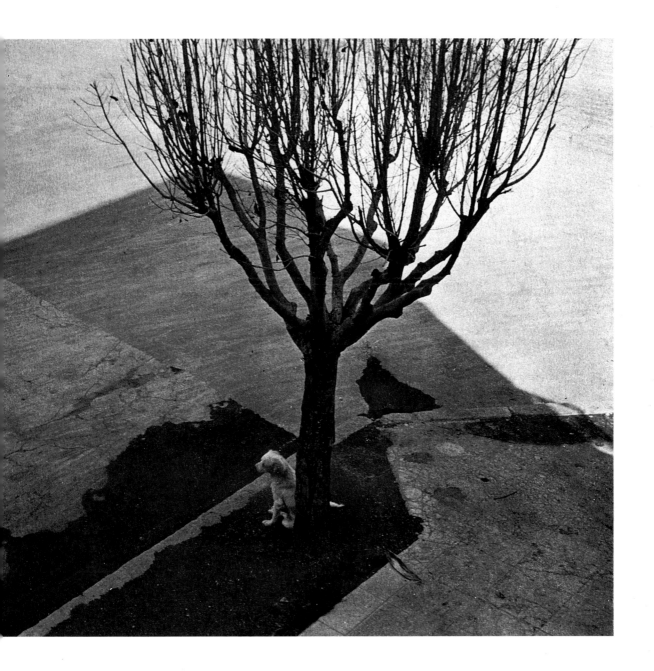

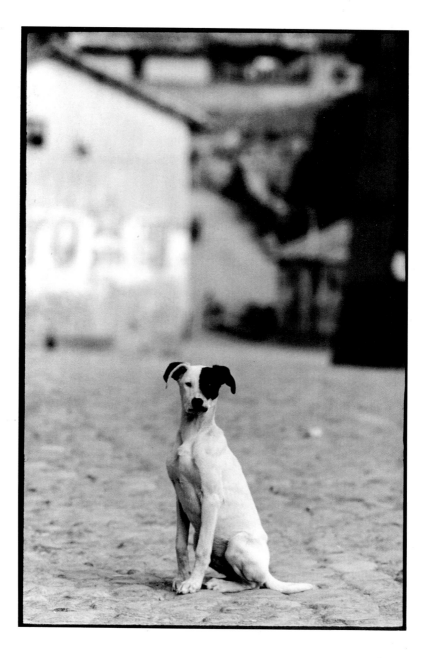

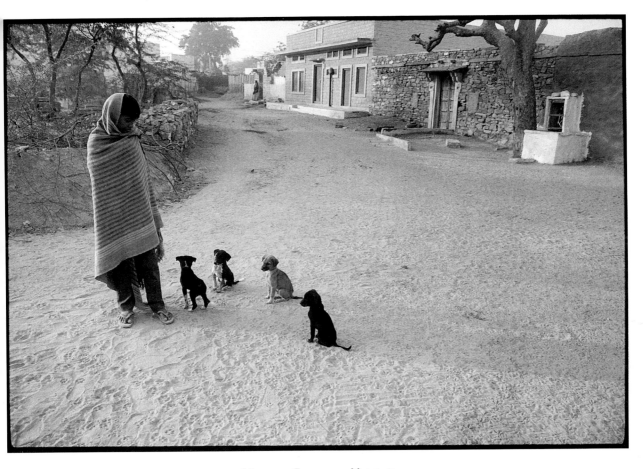

M A R Y E L L E N M A R K
Above: *Jodphur, India,* 1990

■

R O B E R T W H I T M A N
Left: *Sitting Dog,* January 1991

*"While traveling in South America I came to the
outskirts of a village near Ollantaytambo, Peru. A black-and-white
dog appeared and just sat down, her gaze fixed on me,
as if she wanted to block my way."*

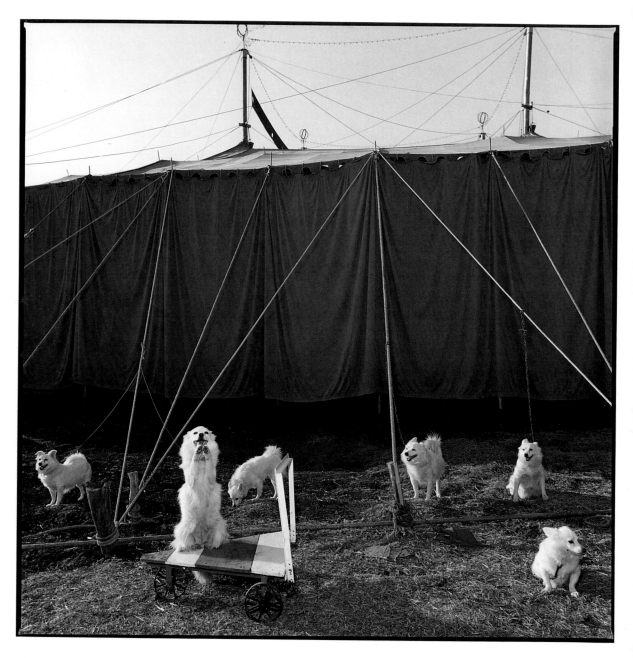

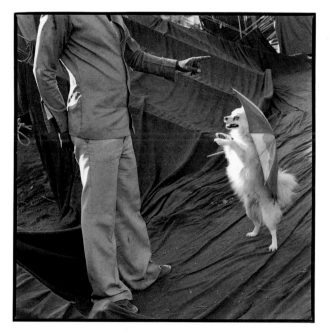

MARY ELLEN MARK
Above: *Ringmaster A. Rehman with His Dog Rosy,*
Great Famous Circus, Calcutta, India, 1989
Left: *Rani Star of the Dog Act, Great Bombay Circus,*
Limbdi, India, 1990

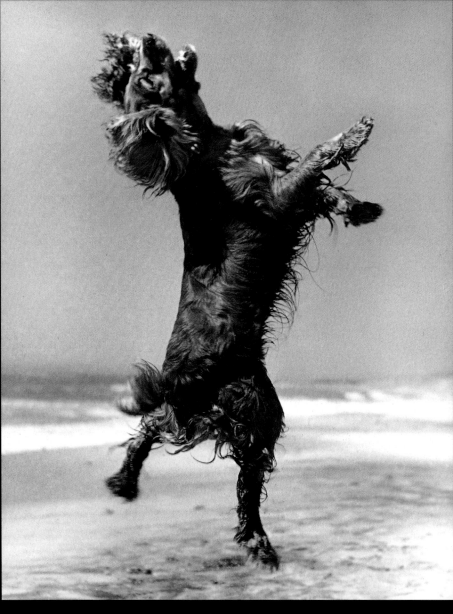

Y L L A

Dog Jumping on the Beach, c. 1944

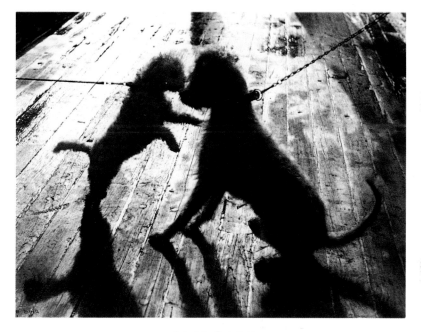

ILSE BING

Shubi Meeting a Girlfriend on the Deck of the Winnipeg, June, 1941

While on board the Winnipeg *fleeing Europe*
for the United States, Bing caught her Airedale about to burst into play.
The dog's nickname was "Mélange d'Amour."

JAMES BARRON
Jeannette, Porto Santo, August 1987

The photographer's wife holds a puppy of the
breed of scrappy hunting dogs native to this barren island far off
the Portuguese coast, near Madeira. Once fertile and lush,
Porto Santo was overrun by rabbits in the fifteenth century after
explorer Bartolomeu Perestrelo let loose a pregnant hare.
The dogs now roam the island as well.

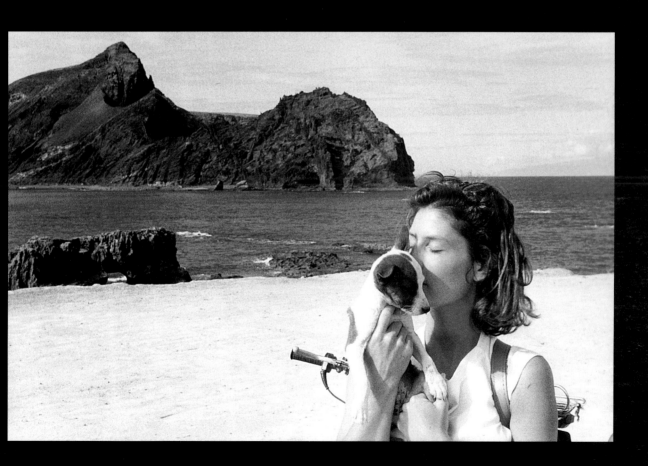

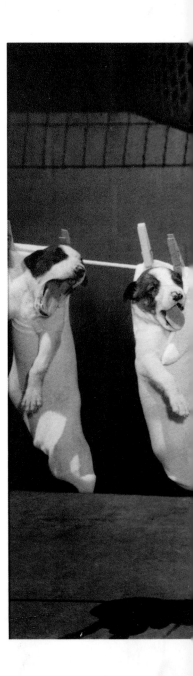

NAT FEIN
The Greyhound Line, New York, c. 1955

A friend's greyhound and her puppies were
enlisted for this gag shot for the New York Herald Tribune.
One of countless human-interest scenarios conceived
by Fein, it took a few tries. After the cupboard to which the clothesline
was suspended crashed to the ground from the weight
of the pups, and the frantic mother was finally calmed down,
the clothesline was tied to a wall.

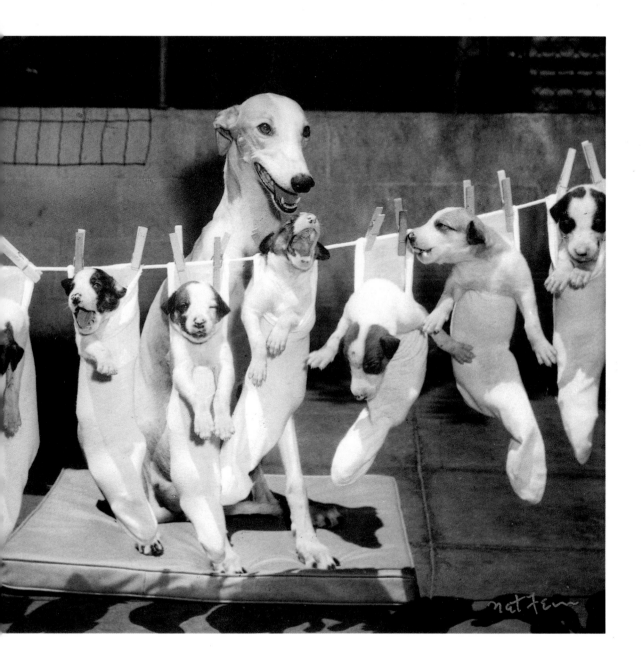

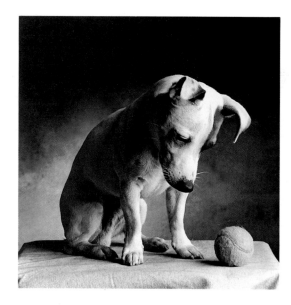

DENIS MOSNER
Above: *Max Contemplating Tennis Ball, New York,* 1991

■

HOWARD BERMAN
Right: *TV Dog,* 1990

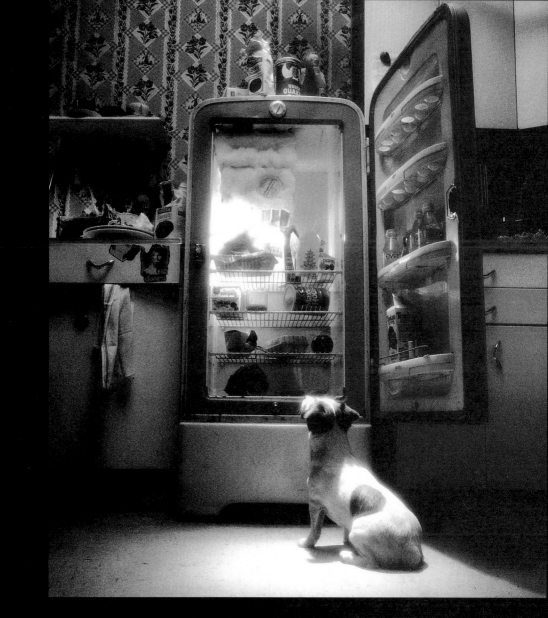

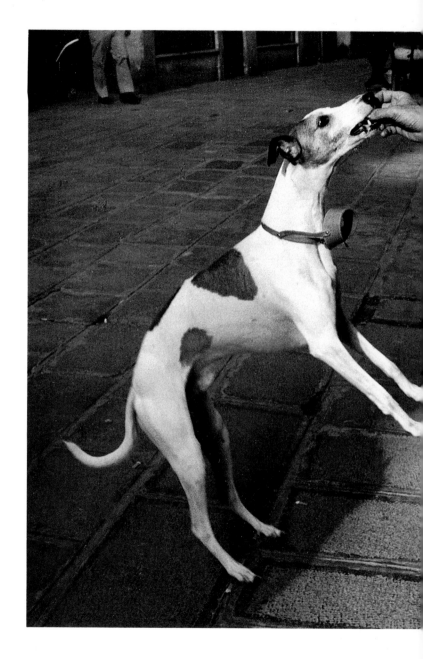

BILL MESSER
The Marbled Paper Maker's Hand,
Venice, 1987

"I had spent all day in
the studio of a paper maker and had just
finished saying goodbye.
I had the impulse to turn around. As I did,
the paper maker reached out of the
doorway to feed his dog a scrap."

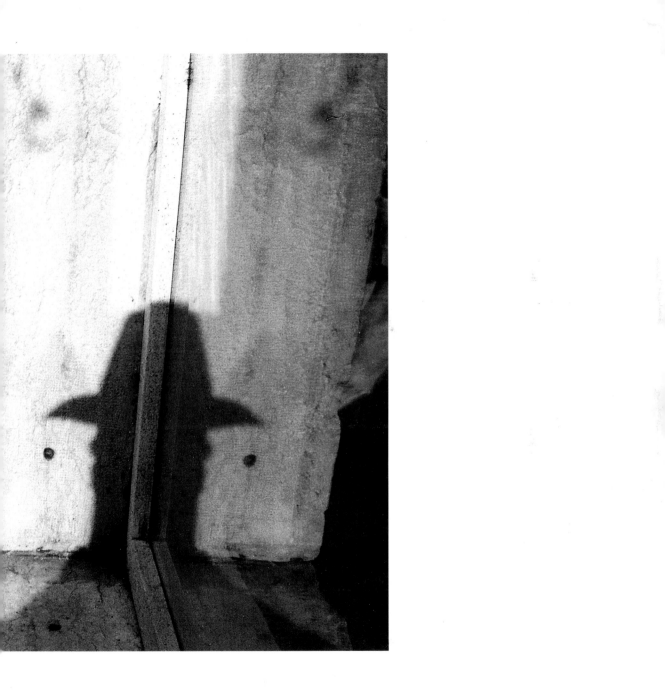

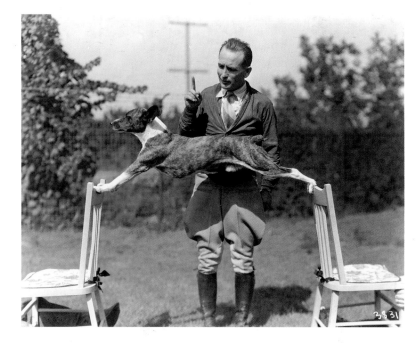

PHOTOGRAPHER UNKNOWN
Above: *A Long Stretch*

A publicity still for a trick dog: "'Buster' of the
Metro-Goldwyn-Mayer 'Barkies' just about doubles his length in this stretching
trick taught him by Rennie Renfro, his trainer."

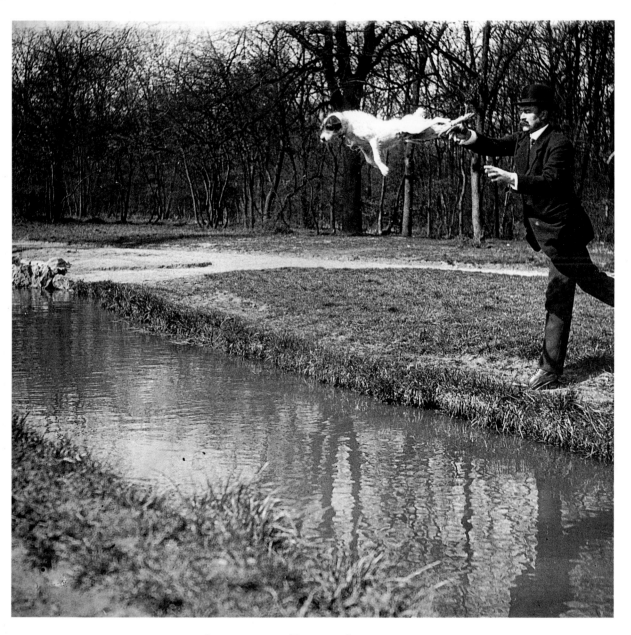

JACQUES-HENRI LARTIGUE
Right: *M. Folletête et Tupy,* Paris, 1912

PHOTOGRAPHER UNKNOWN
Max, Mascot of the 505th Parachute Infantry

The official caption of this army press photograph reads,
"Max is a full-fledged Parachute Trooper, having jumped the necessary five times
to qualify. Max, like all parachutists, was a volunteer."

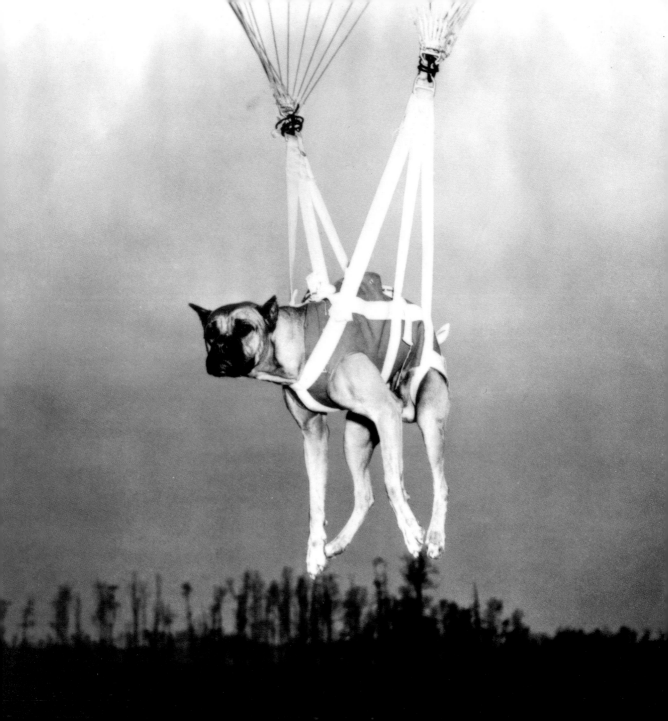

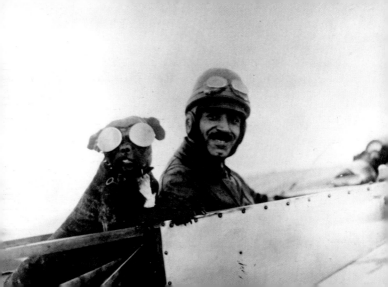

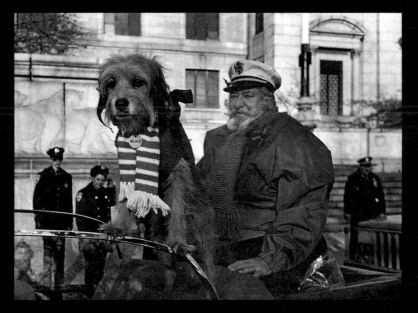

HARVEY STEIN
Untitled, New York, 1982

*Canine movie star Benji takes part in the Macy's
Thanksgiving Day Parade.*

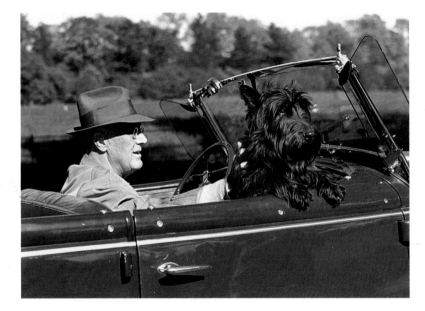

Johnson pulls the ears of one of the White House
beagles, known as Him and Her respectively, while entertaining a group of bankers
on the White House lawn. "The Chief Executive tugged each
of the animals by the ears to arouse yelps, which he said 'does them good'," reported UPI.
"The Chicago Humane Society criticized the president for ear-pulling, saying
it was 'far and away the wrong way' to treat animals."

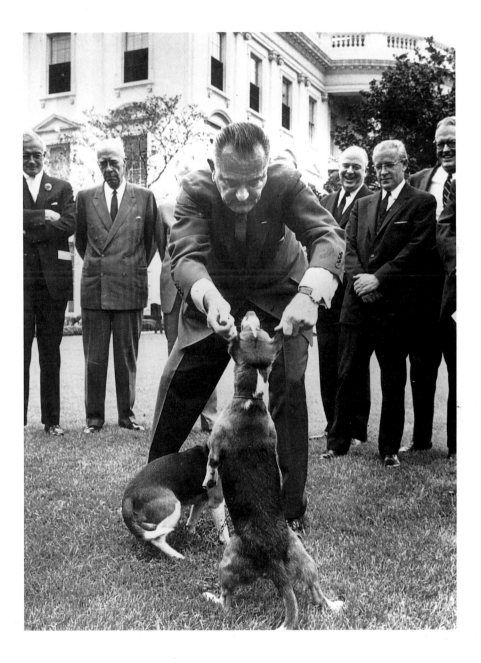

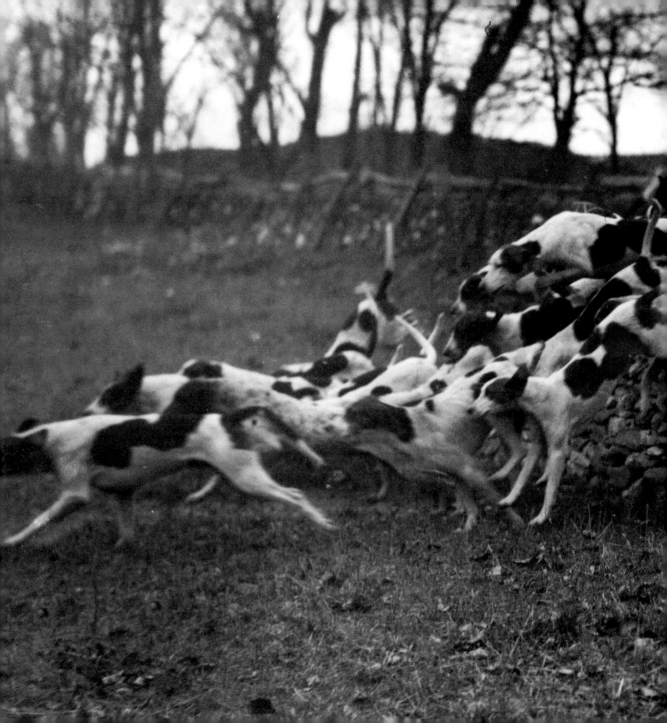

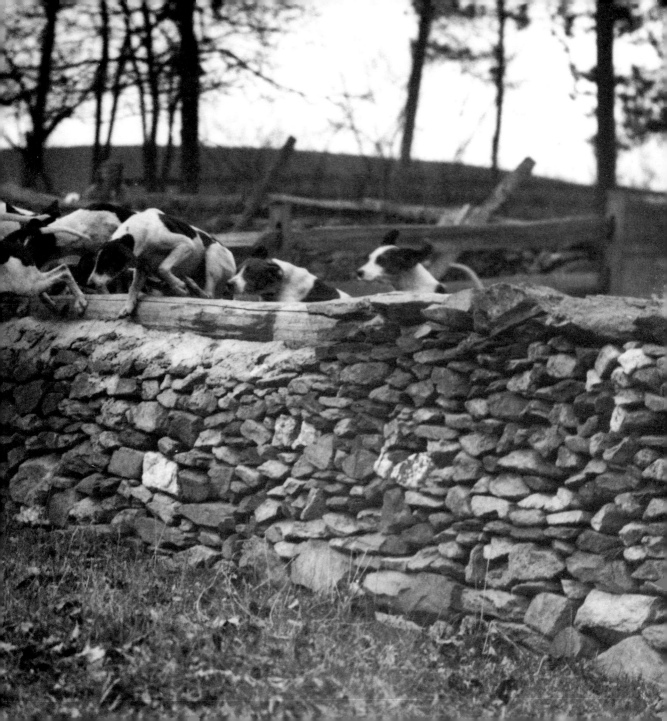

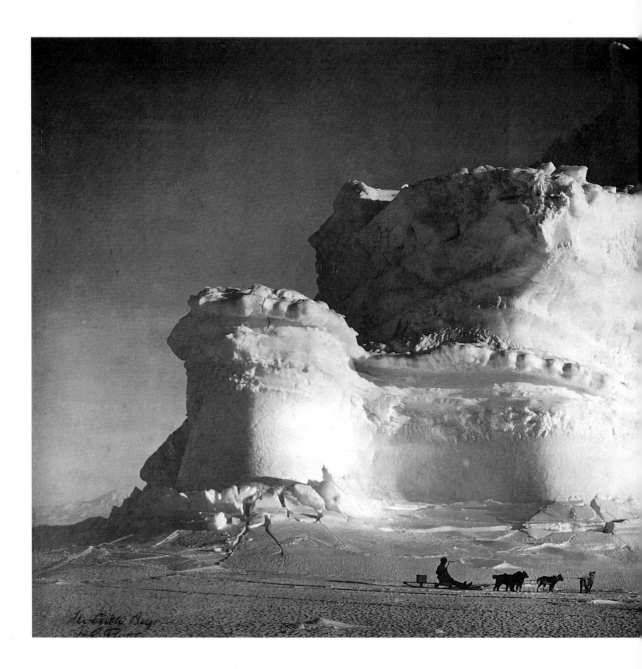

The Castle Berg
Herbert Ponting

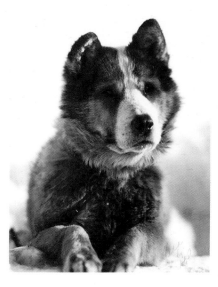

HERBERT GEORGE
PONTING
Above: *Vida, one of the
best dogs used by Capt. Smith on his South
Pole Expedition (1910-1913)*, c.1912
Left: *The Castle Bay*, c. 1912

∎

HAYES
Previous page: *Tally-ho*

*A pack of foxhounds clears a country wall in
one continuous wave.*

HOWARD BERMAN
Family of Dog, 1989

"There were two trainers for nearly each dog,
all standing over my shoulder and calling out different words.
We played musical dogs until I found the right
design and we all needed frequent breaks. In five hours, it was over."
Clockwise from left: golden retriever, American Staffordshire
terrier, beagle, rough-haired collie, Siberian husky, cocker spaniel,
English setter, West Highland white terrier, St. Bernard,
dalmatian, and center, basset hound.

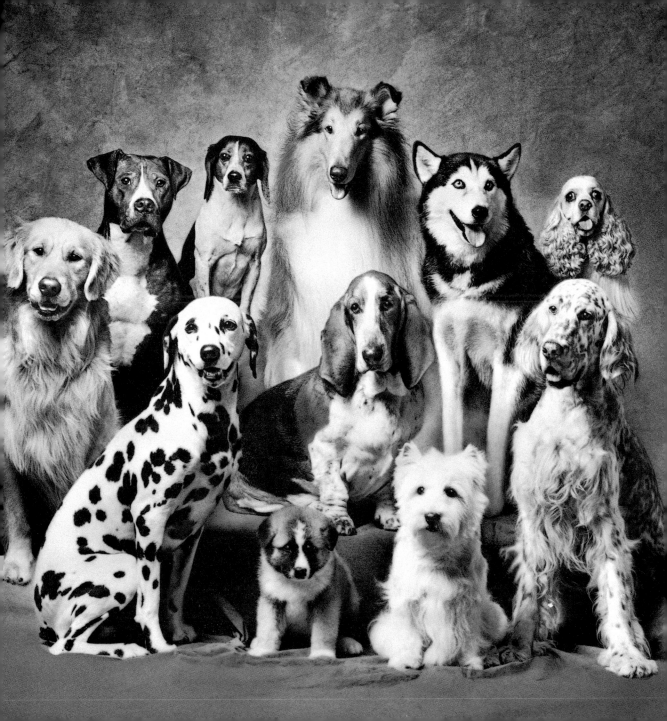

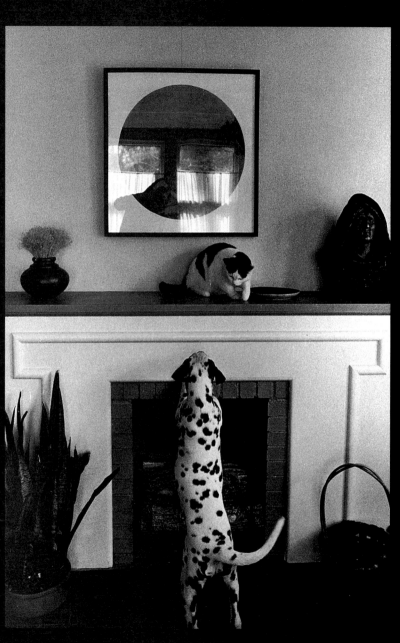

L Y N N L E N N O N
Dalmatian and Cat, c. 1985.

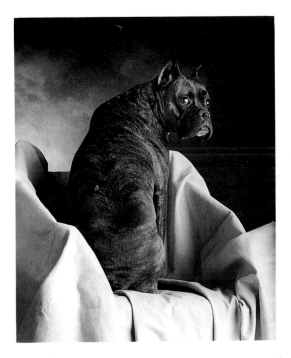

DENNIS MOSNER
Mosca as Gargoyle, New York, 1990

"Photographing my veterinarian's boxers,
Mosca (short for Gittel Moscowitz) and Ethel, convinced me to
get boxers myself. Here we had put Mosca
in the chair. On her own, she sat backwards and cast us this
look over her shoulder."

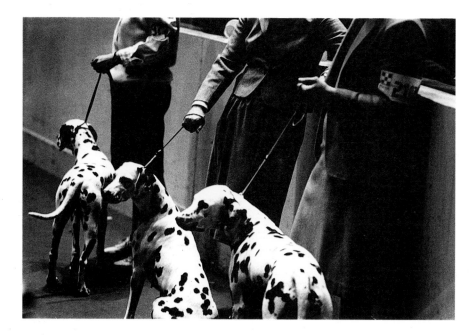

S C O T T H E I S E R
Three Dalmatians, New York, 1986

A trio of dalmatians and their handlers await
their turn in the ring during the non-sporting-breed preliminaries
at the Westminster Kennel Club Dog Show,
Madison Square Garden.

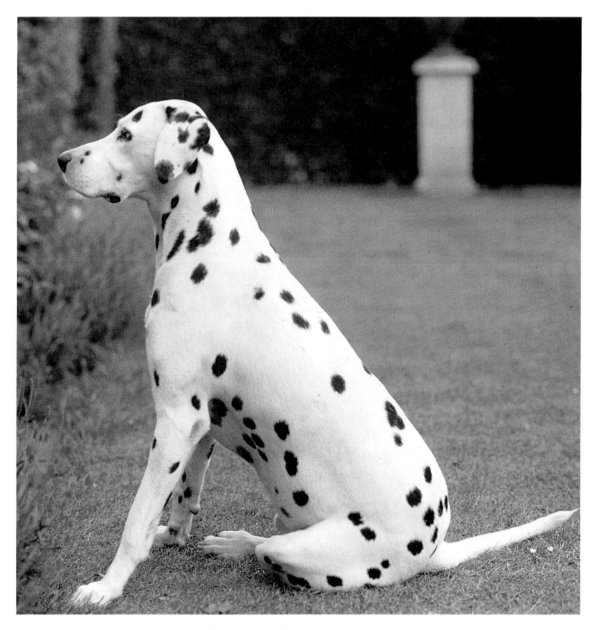

ROBERT MAPPLETHORPE
Dalmatian, 1976

JON FISHER
Twins on a White Bed, New York, 1991

*Unconscious imitators, young whippet siblings Ella and Bosco
adopt twin postures in the studio.*

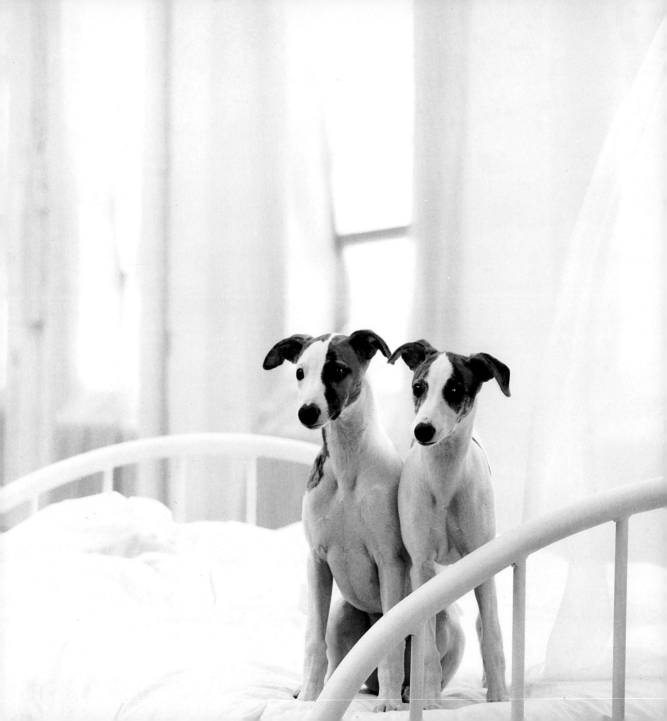

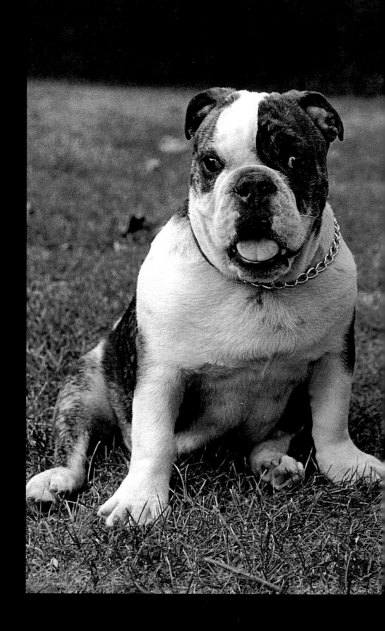

MARY BLOOM
Barney and Sara, 1984

*Barney, an eight-month-old English bulldog
from the Manhattan ASPCA, with Sara Eastright,
the photographer's eight-month-old niece,
in Wilton, Connecticut. "I didn't pose them. They
were just playing together, acting their age,
doing similar things."*

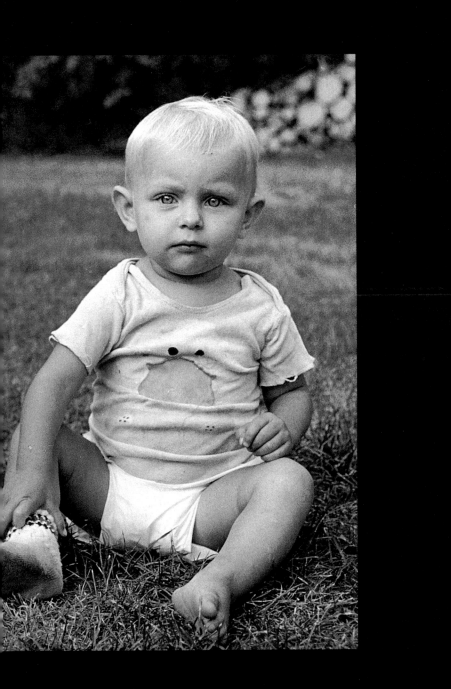

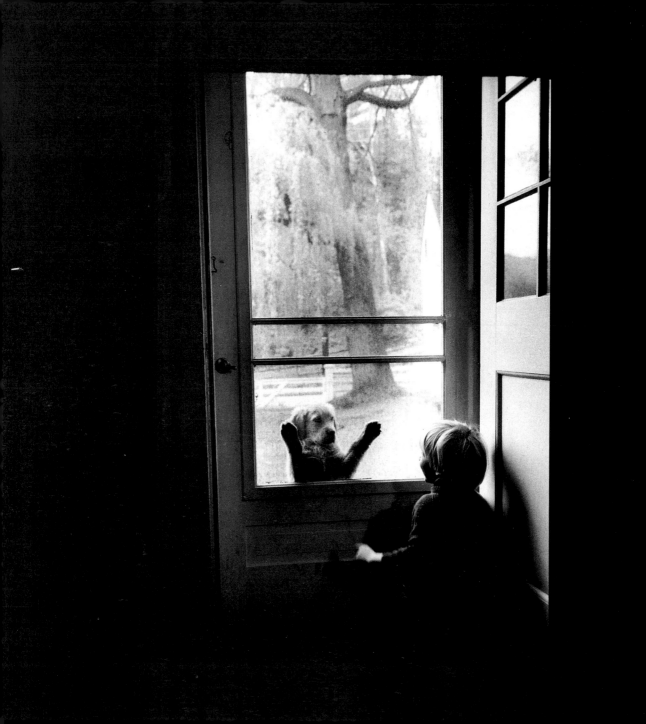

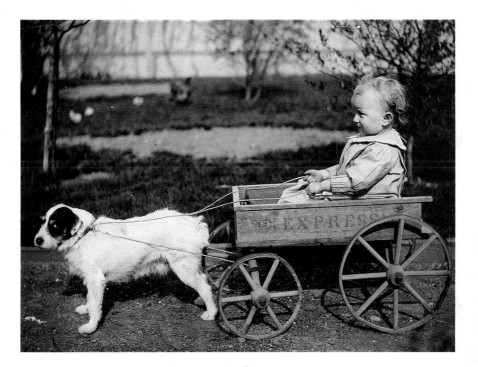

J E A N   B A R N A R D
Above: *The Dog Express,* c. 1910

■

F. W.   B I N Z E N
Left: *Who Wants In?,* c. 1985

*A four-year-old and a puppy consider each
other through the screen door.*

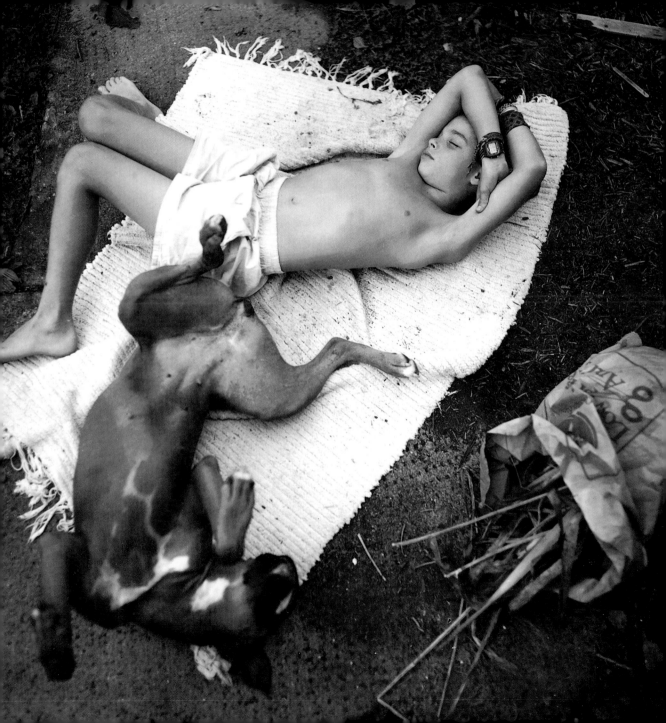

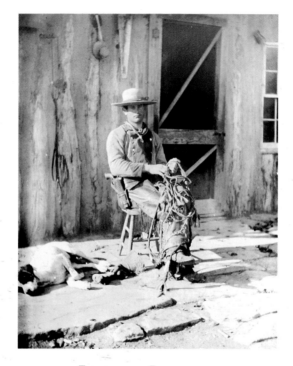

T H O M A S   E A K I N S
Above: *Cowboy Seated in Front of BT Ranch Building,* 1887

■

N A D A R
(G A S P A R D   F E L I X   T O U R N A C H O N)
Right: *Paul and His Dog,* c. 1865

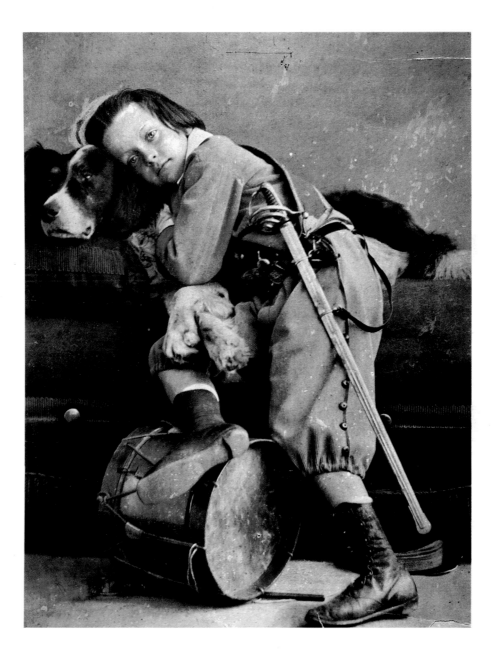

NICHOLAS NIXON
Right: *MDC Park, Allston, Massachusetts,* 1979

Looking out over the water, a weimaraner guards his sunbathing owners.

■

ALLAN JANUS
Following page: *Lucy as Siren,* Dranesville, Virginia, 1985

*A friend's mutt contemplates from the bank of the
Potomac River. "She's not usually this introspective, and her mouth is closed,
which is also unusual. I caught her at a good moment."*

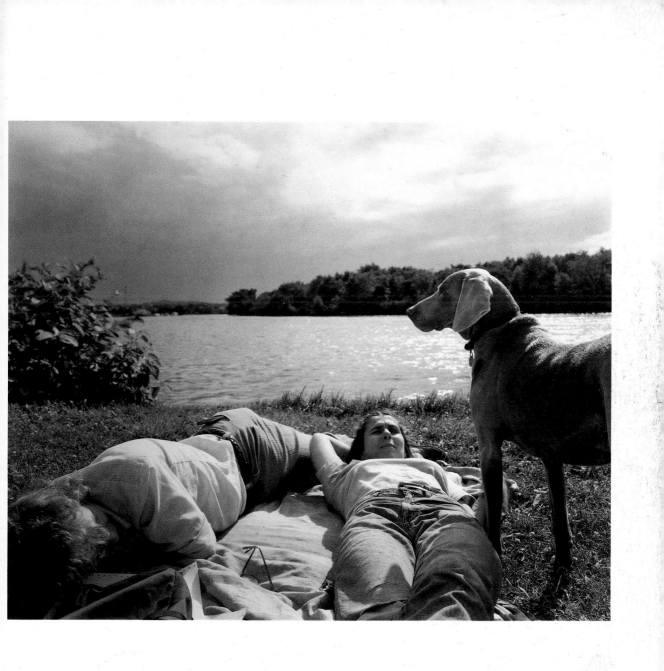

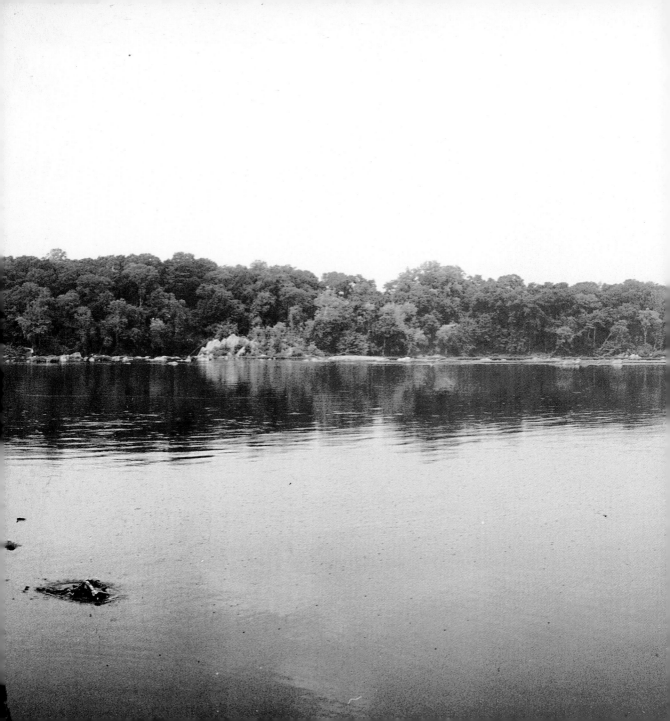

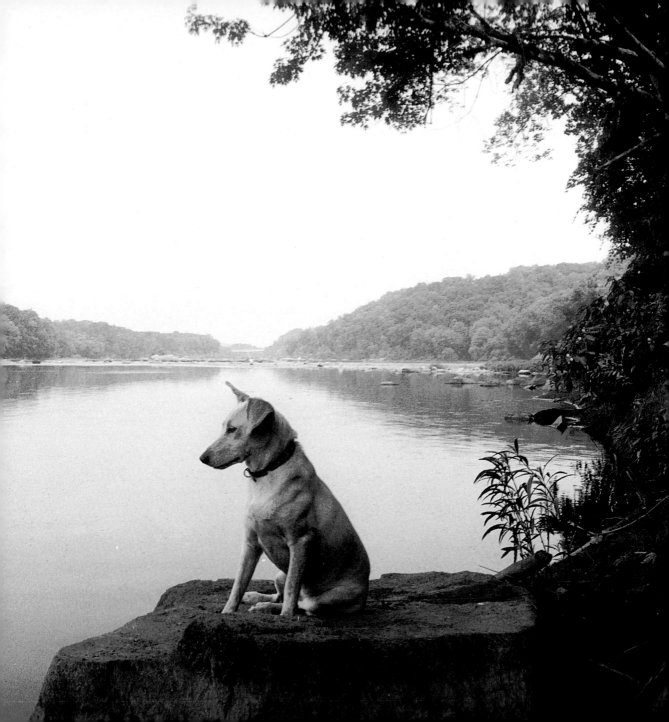

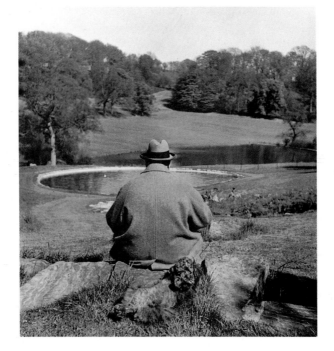

P H I L L I P E H A L S M A N
Above: *Winston Churchill with His Dog Rufus at Chartwell,* England, 1951

"Eventually he reached the end of the garden and sat down on a small rock.
His poodle Rufus installed himself behind Churchill's back."

Right: *Mr. and Mrs. Frederick March Dining with Their Dog,* California, 1950

The Marches and their poodle were photographed for a story called
"How Stars Dine" in McCall's *magazine.*

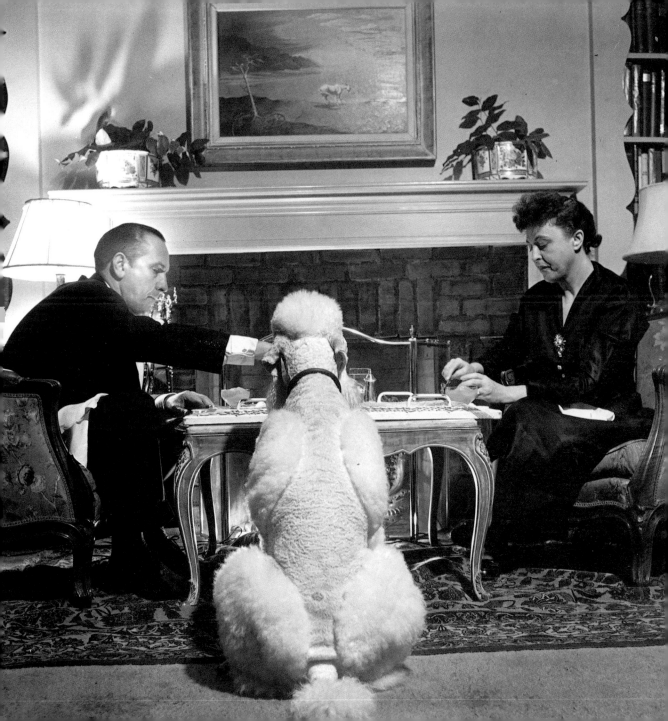

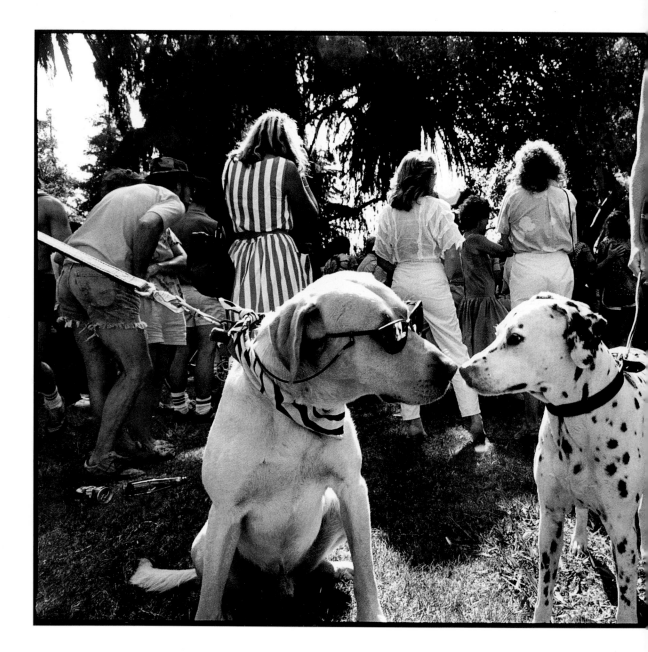

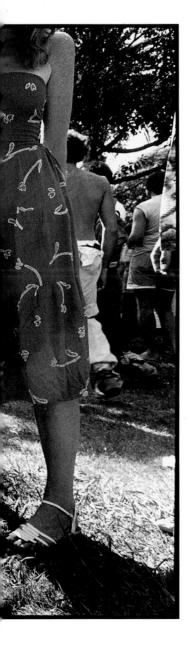

MARY ELLEN MARK
Santa Barbara, California, USA, 1985

WILLIAM WEGMAN
Fay in Boots, New York, 1988

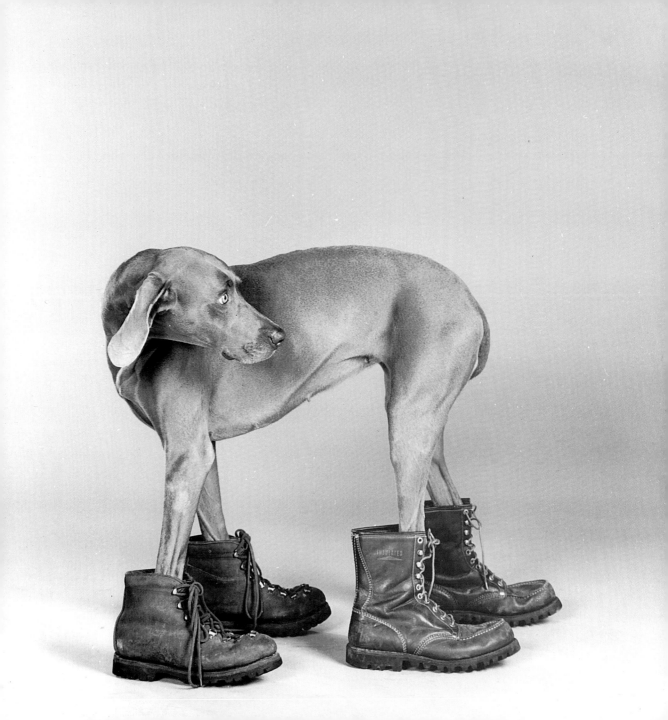

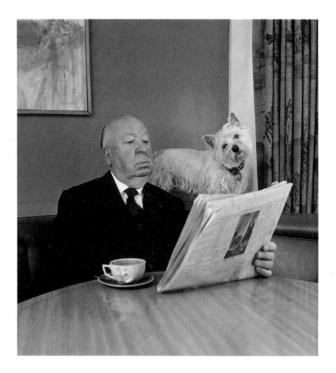

PHILLIPE HALSMAN

Above: *Alfred Hitchcock and His Dog Sarah at Home in
Bel Air, California*, 1974

*"Hitchcock told us two things he was proud of:
that he, his wife, and their dog had consecutive birthdates—
August 12, 13, and 14—and that the dog
always slept on a special pillow between them in their bed. Hitchcock
was 75 years old here. The dog was two
and a half."* —Yvonne Halsman

Right: *Eva Gabor: "Not tonight, Josephine...",* 1953

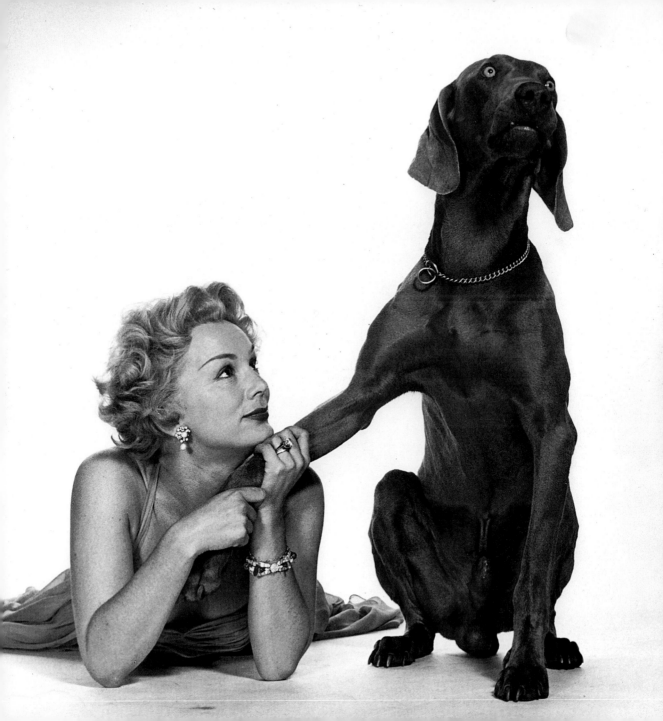

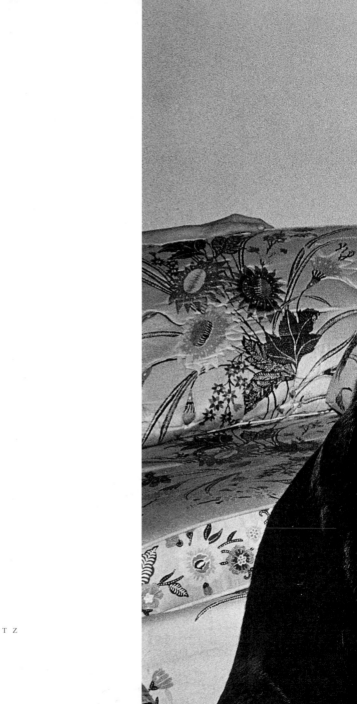

ROBIN SCHWARTZ
Ashley and Rocky, 1987

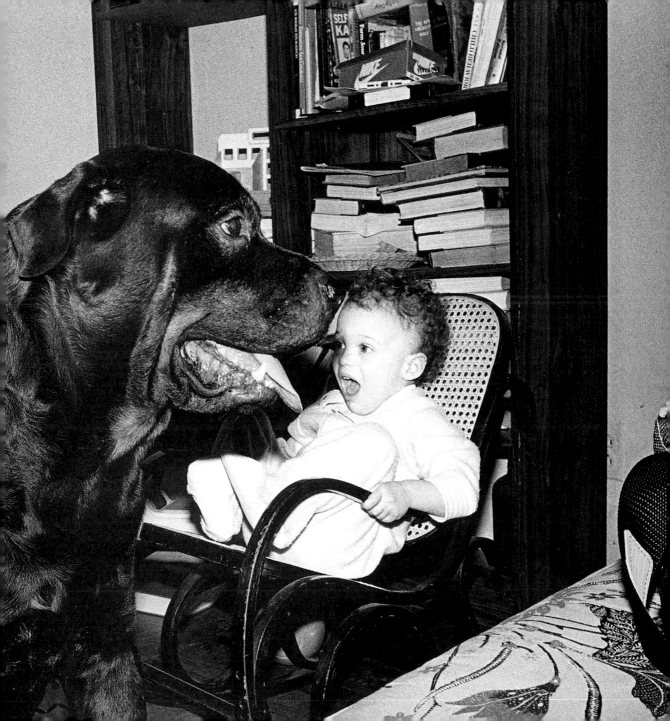

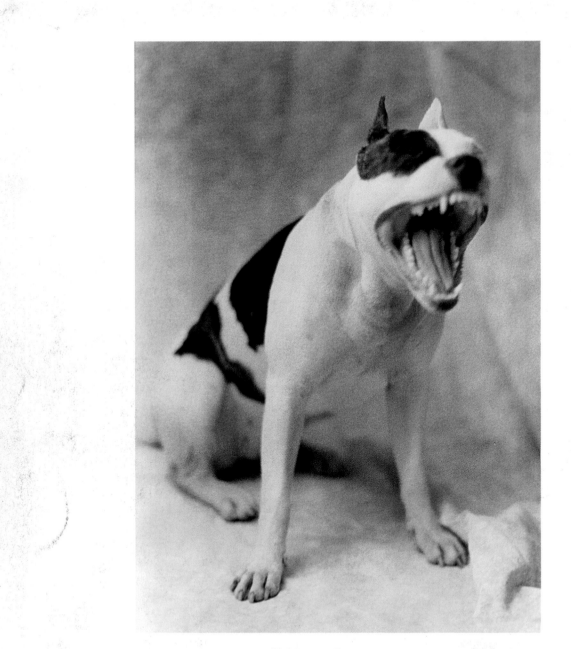

M A R C O   P R O Z Z O
La Chienne Lunatique, New York, February 1991

PHOTOGRAPHIC ACKNOWLEDGMENTS

Front & back covers, 32, 51: © Dennis Mosner

3, 76: © Robin Schwartz

9, 19: © Estate of André Kertèsz

9, 18, 27, 61: Courtesy Houk Friedman
Gallery, New York

11: © 1986 William Clift; courtesy
William Clift

12: © Peter Hujar; courtesy James Danziger
Gallery, New York

13: Reprinted by permission of Joanna T.
Steichen; courtesy the International
Museum of Photography at George Eastman
House, Rochester, New York

14: Courtesy Turner Entertainment Co.

16: © Jean Pigozzi; courtesy Gagosian Gallery,
New York.

19, 20, 46, 47, 63: Courtesy J. Paul Getty
Museum, Malibu, California.

22: © 1991 Robert Whitman

23, 24, 25, 70: © Mary Ellen Mark/Library

26: © 1992 Pryor Dodge; courtesy
Pryor Dodge

29: © 1987 James Barron

33, 49: © Howard Berman

34: © 1987 Bill Messer

36: Courtesy Culver Pictures

37: © Association des Amis de Jacques-Henri
Lartigue; courtesy Monah L. Gettner/
Hyperion Press, New York

39, 40: Courtesy United States Air Force
Collection, National Air and Space Museum

41: © 1982 Harvey Stein

42, 43: Courtesy UPI/Bettman Newsphotos

44: Courtesy Sarah Jeffords Collection

50, 58: Courtesy Photo Researchers

52: © 1986 Scott Heiser

53: © Estate of Robert Mapplethorpe

55: © 1991 Jon Fisher

56: © 1984 Mary Bloom

59: Courtesy Howard Greenberg Gallery, New York

61: © 1989 Sally Mann

62: Courtesy the Pennsylvania Academy of
Fine Arts, Charles Bregler's Thomas Eakins
Collection, purchased with the partial support
of the Pew Memorial Trust

65: © Nicholas Nixon; courtesy Jill Quasha
and Zabriskie Gallery, New York

66: © Allan Janus

68, 69, 75: © Yvonne Halsman

72: © William Wegman; courtesy Pace/McGill
Gallery, New York

78: © 1991 Marco Prozzo

Back flap: © 1989 Priscilla Ratazzi